LONDON ZOO

ART FOR LONDON TRANSPORT

A BOOK OF POSTCARDS

Pomegranate

SAN FRANCISCO

Pomegranate Communications, Inc.
Box 808022, Petaluma CA 94975
800 227 1428; www.pomegranate.com

Pomegranate Europe Ltd.
Unit 1, Heathcote Business Centre, Hurlbutt Road
Warwick, Warwickshire CV34 6TD, UK
[+44] 0 1926 430111; sales@pomeurope.co.uk

ISBN 978-0-7649-6472-5
Pomegranate Catalog No. AA768

Pomegranate publishes books of postcards on a wide range of subjects.
Please contact the publisher for more information.

Cover designed by Ronni Madrid
Printed in Korea
22 21 20 19 18 17 16 15 14 13   10 9 8 7 6 5 4 3 2 1

To facilitate detachment of the postcards from this book, fold each card along its perforation line before tearing.

THE WORLD'S FIRST subterranean railway, the London Underground opened in 1863 and now provides three million rides daily. In 1908, Underground executive Frank Pick began seeking out the country's best artists and designers to produce advertising posters for the expanding transit system. Color printing developments in the last decades of the nineteenth century transformed poster art, and Pick recognized the potential of this graphic medium. The Underground became an important patron of the arts and an acknowledged leader in the field of poster publicity.

For a century, copies of every poster produced for the Underground and its affiliates were kept, and when the collection was transferred to London Transport Museum in the 1980s, it contained more than five thousand printed posters and almost one thousand original artworks. Steadily growing since then, the collection offers a uniquely comprehensive overview of a century of British graphic design. This book of postcards reproduces thirty Underground posters advertising travel to London Zoo—one of the city's favorite public-transport destinations.

Bill Leeson

WE ANIMALS really are well-off in London. Take the London Zoo – smart new Elephant House, brilliant and unconventional new Aviary (not quite finished), classic-of-modern-architecture Penguin Pool, all in the setting of Nash's Regent's Park. Whipsnade's wide open spaces are high on Dunstable Downs – just like home but safer and very much more comfortable. Chessington is more intimate, and caters specially for children. At all three zoos we welcome visitors. They enjoy themselves. And, of course, they interest and amuse us too . . .

Ask for a free 'Know Your Animals' leaflet at any London Transport Enquiry Office

LONDON ZOO

Bill Leeson (b. 1934)
London's Zoos, 1965
Lithograph, 101.6 x 63.5 cm (40 x 25 in.)
Published by London Transport
Collection of London Transport Museum

707 782 9000   WWW.POMEGRANATE.COM

Pomegranate

THE ZOO AQUARIUM is for all who like their fish in untroubled waters. Anglers can watch the famous 44 lb. carp lurching among its more possible cousins. Divers, without fear or equipment, can inspect the life in tropical waters. Sea horse or trout, eel or turtle, your underwater fancy contentedly parades at eye level. *The Zoo and its Aquarium is open every day from 10 to sunset (Sundays 10 to 1.0). Admission 3/- (Sundays 5/-), children half price. The Aquarium costs 1/- extra (children 6d). Underground to Camden Town or Baker Street, then bus 74.*

LONDON ZOO

Hans Unger (German, 1915–1975) and
Eberhard Schulze (German, b. 1938)
The Zoo Aquarium, 1963
Lithograph, 102 x 63.6 cm (40³⁄₁₆ x 25¹⁄₁₆ in.)
Published by London Transport
Collection of London Transport Museum

707 782 9000   WWW.POMEGRANATE.COM

Pomegranate

ZOO AHOY

By **WATERBUS** on the Regent's Canal
Trips hourly from 10 a.m. to 6 p.m. (2 p.m. to
6 p.m. on Sundays) starting from Little Venice.
Buses 6, 18 and 187 go to Little Venice. Or
by Underground to Warwick Avenue, then a short
walk. The starting point is in Delamere Terrace.

By **BUS** on terra firma
Bus 74 passes the gates. Buses 3, 53 and 276
(Mondays to Saturdays) pass within a short walk
of the gates.

By **UNDERGROUND**
to Camden Town or Baker Street then bus 74.

For Whipsnade take a Green Line Coach
726 (limited stop service) from Baker Street

LONDON ZOO

John Burningham (British, b. 1936)
Zoo Ahoy, 1961
Lithograph, 101.6 x 63.5 cm (40 x 25 in.)
Published by London Transport
Collection of London Transport Museum

UNDERGROUND

707 782 9000   WWW.POMEGRANATE.COM

Pomegranate

LONDON ZOO

Shafig Shawki (Sudanese, b. 1923)
London's Open Air; No. 4, Animals, 1948
Lithograph, 101.6 x 63.5 cm (40 x 25 in.)
Published by London Transport
Collection of London Transport Museum

707 782 9000   WWW.POMEGRANATE.COM

Pomegranate

ZOO

STATIONS
REGENTS PARK
CAMDEN TOWN
St JOHNS WOOD

BUS ROUTE No 74

LONDON ZOO

Oleg Zinger (Russian, 1910–1997)
Zoo; Chameleon, 1935
Lithograph, 101.6 x 63.5 cm (40 x 25 in.)
Published by London Transport
Collection of London Transport Museum

WWW.POMEGRANATE.COM

707 782 9000

Pomegranate

DUSK TILL 11 P.M.

THE ZOO BY FLOODLIGHT

UNTIL AUGUST 29 EVERY THURSDAY

ECKERSLEY LOMBERS.

STATIONS – CAMDEN TOWN REGENTS PARK ST. JOHNS WOOD

LONDON ZOO

Tom Eckersley (British, 1914–1997) and
Eric Lombers (British, 1914–1978)
The Zoo by Floodlight, 1935
Lithograph, 25.5 x 30.5 cm (10 1/16 x 12 in.)
Published by London Transport
Collection of London Transport Museum

707 782 9000   WWW.POMEGRANATE.COM

Pomegranate

FOR
THE ZOO

CAMDEN TOWN · REGENT'S PARK
OR CHALK FARM STATION

UNDERGROUND

LONDON ZOO

Maurice A. Miles
For the Zoo, 1934
Lithograph, 101.6 x 63.5 cm (40 x 25 in.)
Published by London Transport
Collection of London Transport Museum

WWW.POMEGRANATE.COM

707 782 9000

Pomegranate

THE ZOO

CAMDEN TOWN, CHALK FARM
OR REGENTS PARK STATION

LONDON ZOO

Oleg Zinger (Russian, 1910–1997)
The Zoo; Lemur, 1933
Lithograph, 101.6 x 63.5 cm (40 x 25 in.)
Published by Underground Electric Railways Company Ltd.
Collection of London Transport Museum

WWW.POMEGRANATE.COM

707 782 9000

Pomegranate

"There's a
Transport of Joy at the Zoo."

Camden Town, Chalk Farm or Regents Park "Underground" Stn.

LONDON ZOO

Jean Dupas (French, 1882–1964)
There's a Transport of Joy at the Zoo, 1933
Lithograph, 101.6 x 63.5 cm (40 x 25 in.)
Published by London Transport
Collection of London Transport Museum

707 782 9000   WWW.POMEGRANATE.COM

Pomegranate

LONDON ZOO

Arnrid Banniza Johnston (Swedish, 1895–1972)
From the Ark to Regent's Park, 1931
Lithograph, 101.6 x 127 cm (40 x 50 in.)
Published by Underground Electric Railways Company Ltd.
Collection of London Transport Museum

UNDERGROUND

707 782 9000   WWW.POMEGRANATE.COM

Pomegranate

UNDERGROUND

THE ZOO

CAMDEN TOWN OR CHALK FARM STNS

LONDON ZOO

F. Gregory Brown (British, 1887–1941)
The Zoo; Aquarium, 1931
Lithograph, 101.6 x 63.5 cm (40 x 25 in.)
Published by Underground Electric Railways Company Ltd.
Collection of London Transport Museum

WWW.POMEGRANATE.COM

707 782 9000

Pomegranate

LONDON ZOO

F. Gregory Brown (British, 1887–1941)
Zoo; Vultures, 1930
Lithograph, 101.6 x 63.5 cm (40 x 25 in.)
Published by Underground Electric Railways Company Ltd.
Collection of London Transport Museum

707 782 9000   WWW.POMEGRANATE.COM

Pomegranate

LONDON ZOO

Arnrid Banniza Johnston (Swedish, 1895–1972)
Regents Park Zoo, 1930
Lithograph, 101.6 x 63.5 cm (40 x 25 in.)
Published by Underground Electric Railways Company Ltd.
Collection of London Transport Museum

707 782 9000 WWW.POMEGRANATE.COM

Pomegranate

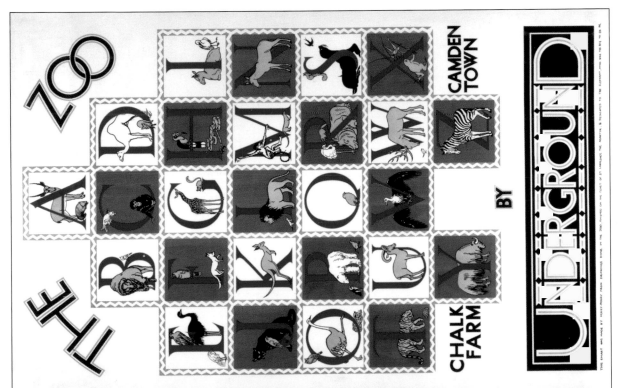

LONDON ZOO

Herry Perry (Heather Perry, British, 1893–1962)
The Zoo, 1928
Lithograph, 101.6 x 63.5 cm (40 x 25 in.)
Published by Underground Electric Railways Company Ltd.
Collection of London Transport Museum

UNDERGROUND

LIVING PICTURES

AT THE ZOO

NEAREST STATIONS CAMDEN TOWN OR CHALK FARM

UNDERGROUND

LONDON ZOO

Small
Living Pictures at the Zoo, 1928
Lithograph, 101.6 x 63.5 cm (40 x 25 in.)
Published by Underground Electric Railways Company Ltd.
Collection of London Transport Museum

WWW.POMEGRANATE.COM

707 782 9000

LONDON ZOO

F. Gregory Brown (British, 1887–1941)
Zoo; Kangaroos, 1927
Lithograph, 101.6 x 63.5 cm (40 x 25 in.)
Published by Underground Electric Railways Company Ltd.
Collection of London Transport Museum

707 782 9000   WWW.POMEGRANATE.COM

Pomegranate

THE ZOO BY **UNDERGROUND**

Living Pictures by Fish and Reptiles,
Manners at meals by Chimpanzees,
Deportment by the Penguins.

REGENTS PARK OR CAMDEN TOWN

LONDON ZOO

Clive Gardiner (British, 1891–1960)
The Zoo; Goats, 1927
Lithograph, 101.6 x 63.5 cm (40 x 25 in.)
Published by Underground Electric Railways Company Ltd.
Collection of London Transport Museum

707 782 9000   WWW.POMEGRANATE.COM

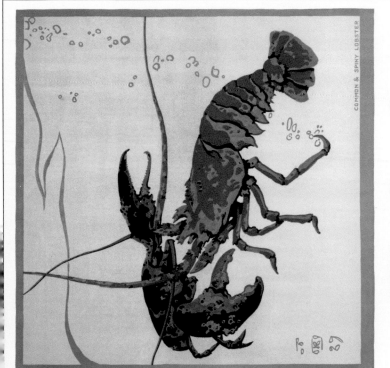

COMMON & SPINY LOBSTER

ZOO

CHALK FARM
CAMDEN TOWN

UNDERGROUND

LONDON ZOO

Richard Barrett Talbot Kelly (British, 1896–1971)
Zoo; Common and Spiny Lobster, 1927
Lithograph, 101.6 x 63.5 cm (40 x 25 in.)
Published by Underground Electric Railways Company Ltd.
Collection of London Transport Museum

707 782 9000   WWW.POMEGRANATE.COM

Pomegranate

THE ZOO BY UNDERGROUND

TO CAMDEN TOWN OR REGENTS PARK STATION

LONDON ZOO

Daphne Barry (British)
The Zoo; Parrot, 1926
Lithograph, 101.6 x 63.5 cm (40 x 25 in.)
Published by Underground Electric Railways Company Ltd.
Collection of London Transport Museum

707 782 9000 WWW.POMEGRANATE.COM

THE ZOO

Book to REGENTS PARK or
CAMDEN TOWN

UNDERGROUND

LONDON ZOO

Gwynedd M. Hudson (British)
The Zoo; Fish, 1926
Lithograph, 101.6 x 63.5 cm (40 x 25 in.)
Published by Underground Electric Railways Company Ltd.
Collection of London Transport Museum

707 782 9000   WWW.POMEGRANATE.COM

FOR THE ZOO

Book to REGENT'S PARK or CAMDEN TOWN

UNDERGROUND

LONDON ZOO

Ruth Sandys
For the Zoo; Sea Lion, 1925
Lithograph, 101.6 x 63.5 cm (40 x 25 in.)
Published by Underground Electric Railways Company Ltd.
Collection of London Transport Museum

UNDERGROUND

ZOO

BOOK TO
CAMDEN TOWN STATION

LONDON ZOO

Sidney Thomas Charles Weeks
Zoo, 1913
Lithograph, 102.2 x 64 cm (40¼ x 25³/₁₆ in.)
Published by Underground Electric Railways Company Ltd.
Collection of London Transport Museum

LONDON ZOO

Reginald Rigby
Off to the Zoo, 1915
Lithograph, 101.6 x 63.5 cm (40 x 25 in.)
Published by Underground Electric Railways Company Ltd.
Collection of London Transport Museum

707 782 9000   WWW.POMEGRANATE.COM

Pomegranate

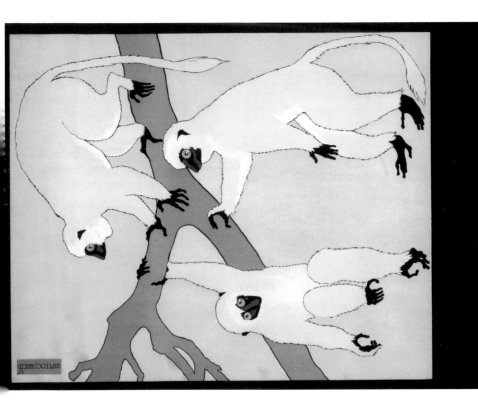

BOOK TO
REGENT'S PARK
OR
CAMDEN TOWN
FOR THE ZOO

LONDON ZOO

Dorothy Burroughes (British, c. 1895–1963)
Book to Regent's Park, 1920
Lithograph, 101.6 x 63.5 cm (40 x 25 in.)
Published by Underground Electric Railways Company Ltd.
Collection of London Transport Museum

707 782 9000   WWW.POMEGRANATE.COM

Pomegranate

LONDON CHARACTERS

THE ZOO KEEPER

— BOOK TO —
REGENTS PARK
or CAMDEN TOWN
— FOR THE ZOO —

.E.A.COX.

LONDON ZOO

Elijah Albert Cox (British, 1876–1955)
London Characters; The Zoo Keeper, 1920
Lithograph, 76.2 x 50.8 cm (30 x 20 in.)
Published by Underground Electric Railways Company Ltd.
Collection of London Transport Museum

FOR THE ZOO, BOOK
TO REGENT'S PARK
OR CAMDEN TOWN

LONDON ZOO

Charles Paine (British, 1895–1967)
For the Zoo, Book to Regent's Park, 1921
Lithograph, 101.6 x 63.5 cm (40 x 25 in.)
Published by Underground Electric Railways Company Ltd.
Collection of London Transport Museum

707 782 9000 WWW.POMEGRANATE.COM

Pomegranate

UNDERGROUND

FOR THE ZOO

BOOK TO
REGENTS PARK OR CAMDEN TOWN
STATIONS.

LONDON ZOO

Dorothy Burroughes (British, c. 1895–1963)
For the Zoo, 1922
Lithograph, 101.6 x 63.5 cm (40 x 25 in.)
Published by Underground Electric Railways Company Ltd.
Collection of London Transport Museum

UNDERGROUND

707 782 9000   WWW.POMEGRANATE.COM

Pomegranate

I AM AT
THE ZOO

BRING ME A FLY.

THE EUROPEAN TREE FROG
(HYLA ARBOREA)

NEAREST STATIONS
REGENTS PARK,
CAMDEN TOWN

LONDON ZOO

J. Martin Pollock
I am at the Zoo; Bring me a Fly, 1923
Lithograph, 101.6 x 63.5 cm (40 x 25 in.)
Published by Underground Electric Railways Company Ltd.
Collection of London Transport Museum

WWW.POMEGRANATE.COM

707 782 9000

Pomegranate

UNDERGROUND

REGENTS PARK

FOR THE ZOO

FOR THE ROYAL
BOTANIC GARDENS

Book to
Camden Town or
Regents Pk Stations

Book to
Regents Park
Station

LONDON ZOO

Mrs. G. Barraclough
Regents Park for the Zoo, 1923
Lithograph, 101.6 x 63.5 cm (40 x 25 in.)
Published by Underground Electric Railways Company Ltd.
Collection of London Transport Museum

707 782 9000   WWW.POMEGRANATE.COM

Pomegranate

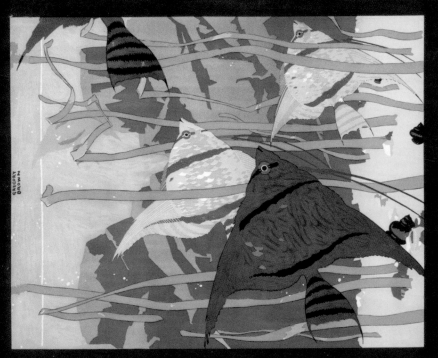

THE ZOO

Book to REGENT'S PARK or CAMDEN TOWN

UNDERGROUND

LONDON ZOO

F. Gregory Brown (British, 1887–1941)
The Zoo, 1924
Lithograph, 101.6 x 63.5 cm (40 x 25 in.)
Published by Underground Electric Railways Company Ltd.
Collection of London Transport Museum

WWW.POMEGRANATE.COM

707 782 9000

Pomegranate